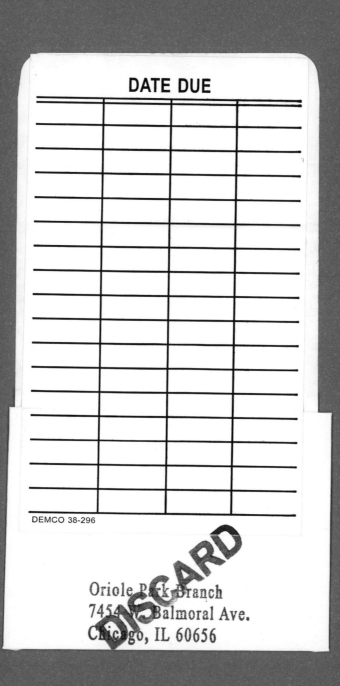

DATE DUE

DEMCO 38-296

LOOKING FOR JAGUAR

and Other Rain Forest Poems

LOOKING FOR JAGUAR

and Other Rain Forest Poems

BY **Susan Katz**

PICTURES BY **Lee Christiansen**

Greenwillow Books, *An Imprint of HarperCollinsPublishers*

Contents

Looking for Jaguar · 6

Nightmares Tonight · 8

Giant Armadillo · 9

Jungle Concert · 10

Soooo Sloow · 12

Walking Tree · 13

Cloud Forest · 14

Anaconda · 16

Piranhas · 17

In the Flooded Forest · 19

Jungle Lunes · 20

Panther Chameleon • 21

Okapi • 22

SSSSSSnake • 23

Twelve Inches High • 24

Rainbow Lorikeets • 26

Rafflesia • 28

Tiger Passes • 31

Canopy • 32

About the Poems • 34

About the Rain Forest • 38

Looking for Jaguar

The darkness seems alive—it watches us.
Though almost no one sees him here,
We listen for the jaguar's grunting call,
Shadowed by leaves like feathers, ribbons, fans.

Though almost no one sees him here,
We look for tawny fur, black spots and rings.
Shadowed by leaves like feathers, ribbons, fans,
A stream is greeny dark beside the path.

We look for tawny fur, black spots and rings.
Where purple flowers float like butterflies,
A stream is greeny dark beside the path.
The air's so hot and wet it's hard to breathe.

Where purple flowers float like butterflies,
We listen for the jaguar's grunting call.
The air's so hot and wet it's hard to breathe.
The darkness seems alive—it watches us.

Nightmares Tonight

A hairy bird-eating spider,
big as my fist,
with fangs poking from brown fur muffs,
stares at me with eight glittery eyes.
I'm going to have nightmares tonight.

An eyelash viper,
yellow as buttered corn,
with stubby horns above its eyes,
opens wide its fanged pink mouth.
I'm going to have nightmares tonight.

An upside-down brown bat,
hanging like a leather coat,
with squished-in face and vampire teeth,
sleeps in a hollow tree till dark.
I think I'll just stay awake.

Giant Armadillo

Rat-tailed, pig-nosed, rabbit-eared fellow
Stuck in a turtle shell, poor armadillo.
Warts on his tongue and plates on his back.
Maggots and worms are his favorite snack.
He's a snuffler and snorter instead of a squeaker.
Often he smells like a very old sneaker.
He wears on one toe the world's largest claw,
So you'd think that everyone might stand in awe,
But he hides in a hole if someone says *boo*.
I wish I could tell him, "There's *no one* like you!"
With a hundred-tooth smile and his own suit of armor,
He's really a one-in-a-million-y charmer.

Jungle Concert

I roam through green silence,
then stop
                     to let blossoms of sound
unfold in many colors:

rustles in the underbrush,
crinkle of leaves as a monkey lands,
a jagged whistle cutting the air,

twee twee twee whit trickling down
                                   from a tree,
a parrot's *raak kraak kwaaa*,
the chirps and whirrs of insects and frogs,

a noise like distant barks of a dog
becoming the roar
                           of a dozen winds
as howler monkeys cry.

Last the *whish* and spatter of rain
filling my ears,
                       filling the world
with no other sound but water.

Soooo Sloow

With algae green in his shaggy hair,
A sloth overhead is going somewhere.

Traveling upside down by hooks on his toes,
He slowly turns his head as he goes.

He's the pokiest fellow you're likely to meet;
In an hour, if rushed, he might move fifteen feet.

He can spend a month digesting his dinner
(Though he never seems to get any thinner).

Hook by hook, toe by toe,
He just doesn't move any faster than sloow.

Where he's going now I haven't been told,
But before he arrives, we may both be old.

Walking Tree

More than anything else, I think I'd like
To watch this palm setting out on a hike.

Its long, skinny trunk isn't planted in ground,
So (unlike other trees) it can walk around.

Instead of legs, it grows roots like stilts,
And it edges along as each of them wilts.

Yet I've stood here peering for half a day,
And even the fronds at the top didn't sway.

I can't see it move though I stare and stare,
But ten years from now, it will be over there.

Cloud Forest

Mist blows through a gap in the trees,
And mosses hang like ragged beards.

Deep in the shadows, owl eyes peer.
—No, it's only a butterfly.

Fog drifts like curtains of gauze,
And vines creep through twisted trees.

Somewhere a *bonk* like a haunted clock.
—No, it's only a bellbird's cry.

A frog on a leaf, porcelain bright,
Winks its eye and seems to smile.

Shadows and mist, ghosts and fog.
—Real bird, real butterfly, real frog.

Anaconda

As the snake moves in and out of himself,
Part of him writes a word, another part erases it.

Spots, rings, lines, and black eyes—hardly visible,
A patch of dappled shadows by the water.

An uncoiled rope stretched out along the stream,
He's as long as a bus, as wide as a telephone pole.

The larger he gets, the fewer enemies he has;
His hunger swallows tapirs, turtles, caimans, even humans.

Silently he glides away, a ripple in shadowed water,
Erasing all of himself except the shiver down my spine.

Piranhas

When I look at them, I see:
scaly, blue bulldogs,
really mad pancakes,
the blades of two hundred curved saws,
bear traps made of teeth,
reasons not to go swimming.
And when they look at me,
they see: school lunch!

In the Flooded Forest

The river carries us to the sky,
Where a tiny catfish spends its life in a tree.
Neon tetras dart among leaves,
And a sting ray ripples beneath a branch.

We paddle through the treetops
Past a colony of dangling, woven nests.
Orchids grow within our grasp,
And a monkey leans from a nearby limb to spy.

Here we see the forest twice.
Banana blossoms kiss their own reflections.
A dolphin leaps past a parrot's perch
As we drift between the worlds.

Jungle Lunes

LIANA

Above our heads
Liana blossoms glimmering, pink stars
In green sky.

BANANA LEAF

Furry golf balls
Hang underneath a drooping leaf,
White bats asleep.

Panther Chameleon

A little dragon sways along a branch,
then stops,
its feet clinging like green clamps.

Its head, flat body, and curlicue tail
are green.
That means it's happy.

So close I can see its sleepy-looking eyes,
I pause.
One eye swivels backward.

On a neighboring branch, a butterfly lands,
yellow bright.
Oh, look out, butterfly!

Too late.
A long, sticky tongue shoots up. *Zap!*
Butterfly for breakfast.

Okapi

A dark brown horse
whose hind end
wears zebra stripes,

its neck too short
for a giraffe,
too long for anything else,

with big cow ears,
soft cow nose,
and giraffe's velvet horns,

this animal's
a jigsaw puzzle
put together wrong.

SSSSSSnake

Lean, leaf-green,
Black bead eyes.
Twines in vines,
Loops and ties.
Kinky, slinky.
—This boy spies.
Coiling, roiling.
—"Hey!" he cries.
Boa? Noa!
Can't be that.
Mamba? Scramba!
Leaves his hat.

Twelve Inches High

Royal antelope,
the size of a pet cat,
with legs thin as a pencil,
hides in the bushes,
timid and cinnamon furred,
so small
he can easily dodge
through the densest jungle,
nine feet at a bound.

Goliath frog,
the size of a pet cat,
with legs strong as a wrestler's,
squats by the river,
mute and slippery skinned,
so big
she can easily leap
across the swiftest rapids,
ten feet at a hop.

Rainbow Lorikeets

Come to this place every day.
Hold still;
           don't breathe.
A little dish of honey
can call a rainbow close.
Thump,
       thump,
             thump,
                  thump.
Four in a row, they land.

Blue heads cluster,
              tip of each tongue
a fringed brush
          to lap honey up.

Move a step nearer every day.
Hold still;
           don't breathe.
Close,
      close,
         closer
            they land.
One day a rainbow with wings
may light on your arm.

Rafflesia

World's biggest flower, the giant rafflesia
Isn't a plant that tries hard to please ya.
Inside a vine, it grows from a thread
To be three feet across, a speckled bright red,
And sends out the fragrance of something quite dead,
Which gives it the nickname of stinking corpse lily.
It scatters its four million seeds willy-nilly
Till a pale orange cabbage (a bud in disguise)
Bursts through the vine, grows to basketball size
(To the vast admiration of beetles and flies),
And finally opens up with a hiss.
This is a flower you might want to miss.

Tiger Passes

Soft feet pad in the leaves.
Molasses stripes of sun and shade,
tiger passes.
He doesn't even glance my way.

With pink tongue, amber eyes,
his tail curled up at the end,
tiger passes.
He glides, flows, anything but walks.

Canopy

We stand at the top of the world
In a garden of flowers high in the air.
Among the billowing waves of green,
Bluebirds and hornbills feast on yellow figs.

In a garden of flowers high in the air,
A flying dragon glides like a purplish kite.
Bluebirds and hornbills feast on yellow figs
While honeybees hum in the Tualang tree.

A flying dragon glides like a purplish kite.
Oh, how I'd love to lift my arms and soar
While honeybees hum in the Tualang tree!
Here even snakes can ribbon through the air.

Oh, how I'd love to lift my arms and soar
Among the billowing waves of green!
Here even snakes can ribbon through the air.
We stand at the top of the world.

About the Poems

"Looking for Jaguar": The *jaguar*, found in Central and South America, is not only a skilled climber, runner, and swimmer, but also a clever hunter, even known to catch fish by dangling its tail into the water as bait.

"Nightmares Tonight": All the creatures in this poem range through the rain forests of northern South America. The *bird-eating spider*, despite its name, is more likely to eat small mammals and reptiles than birds. The *eyelash viper* does eat birds, catching them by concealing itself among flowers. *Vampire bats*, of course, live on a diet of blood, which they lap with grooved tongues. Human toes, noses, and ears are among this bat's favorite targets, but it only drinks about two tablespoons of blood a day.

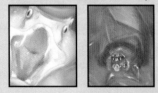

"Giant Armadillo": The *giant armadillo*, found in South America, can grow to four or five feet long and weigh up to 130 pounds. When frightened, it takes only two minutes to dig a hole to hide in; there it braces itself and can be pulled out only with great effort.

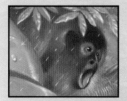

"Jungle Concert": While it's often difficult to see rain-forest dwellers, it's usually easy to hear them. *Howler monkeys*, the noisiest residents of South American rain forests, emit roaring howls which can be heard two miles away.

"Soooo Sloow": The *sloth*, widespread throughout Central and South America, lives even in the flooded forest where, being an excellent swimmer, it travels by water from tree to tree.

"Walking Tree": The *Amazonian walking palm* is rooted in the ground not by its trunk but by a circle of tall, thin stilt roots. Periodically these "stilts" die off and are replaced by new ones, which always root themselves toward sunlight; in the course of a decade, the palm can actually "walk" ten feet or so to a sunnier location.

"Cloud Forest": *Cloud forests* occur throughout the tropics wherever rain forests grow so high up on mountainsides that clouds actually drift among the trees. Cloud forests are notable for their cool temperature (fifty to sixty-five degrees Fahrenheit) and their lushness (nearly all the trunks and branches of the trees are covered with such plants as mosses, ferns, and orchids). The eye pattern on the *owl butterfly*'s wings scares off predators. The owl butterfly, *three-wattled bellbird*, and many species of frog are found in the Monteverde cloud forest of Costa Rica.

"Anaconda": The South American *anaconda*, the world's largest snake, is usually found near rivers or streams, where it ambushes prey.

"Piranhas": Some species of *piranha* are highly aggressive; attacking in schools of hundreds of fish, they can devour a cow in minutes. Other piranha species, however, are peaceable fish that primarily eat fruit. Both kinds are found in the Amazon River.

"In the Flooded Forest": In the *flooded forest* of the Amazon, thousands of square miles of rain forest are covered by as much as forty to fifty feet of river water for as long as ten or eleven months of the year. Both land and water creatures have adapted to this river among the treetops.

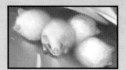

"Jungle Lunes": *Flowering lianas* are found in all tropical rain forests. Over eight hundred varieties of *banana plants* are also widely distributed. *White tent-making bats*, found in Central and northern South America, make shelters under large leaves by chewing through leaf veins on both sides of the midrib so the leaf collapses into a tent.

"Panther Chameleon": The *panther chameleon*, found in Madagascar, uses its ability to change color in fifteen seconds as a way of expressing emotions. Green when it's happy, it fades to tan if tired or ill and turns yellow when it feels like giving up. If it gets mad, bright stripes appear, and when it loses its temper completely, it turns black.

"Okapi": A resident of African rain forests, the odd-looking *okapi*, though known by indigenous people for centuries, was believed by European explorers to be a mythical animal until the early 1900s, when an okapi was finally "discovered" by Sir Harry Johnston.

"SSSSSSnake": While the *green mamba* and *emerald tree boa* are both green snakes, easily camouflaged in the trees, the boa lives in South America, far from the mamba, which belongs to the most poisonous group of snakes in Africa.

"Twelve Inches High": The *goliath frog* and the *royal antelope* are rare species found only in limited ranges, each in a different part of west Africa. The antelope evolved into a dwarf so it could travel more easily through dense undergrowth, while the cold-blooded frog was able to evolve into a giant because of the constantly warm climate.

"Rainbow Lorikeets": Found in Australia and New Guinea, *rainbow lorikeets* are among the least timid of rain-forest creatures. In jungle parks or preserves, where the birds come into daily contact with visitors, lorikeets sometimes become so tame that they follow people into campers in hopes of a bread-and-honey treat.

"Rafflesia": The *rafflesia*, found in parts of Malaysia and Indonesia, is a parasite which grows inside a vine. A rafflesia has no roots, leaves, or stem, but its flower can weigh more than thirty pounds and holds several gallons of a foul-smelling nectar highly appealing to beetles and flies.

"Tiger Passes": *Tigers* live in rain forests in parts of Asia, including India, Indochina, and Sumatra. In Bangladesh people working in the jungle sometimes wear masks on the backs of their heads so a tiger coming up behind them will think they're watching it and won't pounce.

"Canopy": All these plants and animals live in the world's highest and densest canopy, located on the island of Borneo in Malaysia. The *Tualang* is the tallest known rain-forest tree. Flocks of *fairy bluebirds* and various species of *hornbills* feast in the canopy's fig trees. Many canopy residents travel by air: the *flying dragon* glides by spreading out a loose membrane of skin that forms a wing on each side, and *flying snakes* flatten their bodies like ribbons and "swim" through the air.

About the Rain Forest ▲ ▲ ▲ ▲ ▲ ▲ ▲ ▲ ▲ ▲ ▲ ▲ ▲ ▲ ▲

Tropical rain forests are found in a belt around the earth's equator, in parts of Central and South America, Africa, southeast Asia, Australia, and various tropical islands. Sunlight in the rain forest lasts for nearly twelve hours every day all year, and in the wettest rain forests (those closest to the equator), it rains nearly every day, often in spectacular cloudbursts. The year-round temperature averages seventy-five to eighty degrees Fahrenheit, and the humidity seldom falls below 95 percent.

All tropical rain forests are fundamentally similar, though they fall into different categories depending on their altitude, rainfall, and soil. The two basic types are *lowland forests*, which are the most common, and *montane forests*, which grow on mountains. Some lowland forests grow so close to rivers or to the ocean that they're flooded for part of every year, and some montane forests grow so high that they're shrouded in clouds.

All rain forests consist of a series of layers. At the very top, fifteen stories above the ground, a few giant trees form the *emergent layer*. Beneath them, the rest of the full-grown trees, which shoot straight up toward the sun seventy feet or higher before they branch out, create a tightly woven tangle of branches known as the *canopy*. Most jungle flowers and fruits, and the creatures that feed on them, are found in this high, airy, sun-drenched layer.

Because the canopy is so thick, only 2 percent or less of the sun's light can pass through it. At ground level, therefore, the rain forest is a dark, hot, humid place, much less crowded than many people imagine. The smaller plants that grow there, such as seedlings, saplings, ferns, shrubs, and a few scattered herbs and grasses, form the layer called the *understory*. The very bottom layer, the *forest floor*, is actually bare in spots except for a thin covering of rotting plant debris, which falls from the trees above and is broken down by insects, fungi, and other species that feed on decaying vegetation.

Weaving these layers together are several kinds of plants that grow on and among the trees. Woody *lianas* and other climbing plants grow upward from the forest floor, often flowering in the canopy. *Epiphytes*—plants such as orchids, which do not root in the ground but get their food from rainwater and plant debris—grow on branches, trunks, and even one another. A few plants, such as the strangler fig, are parasites that smother the tree on which they live and take over its place in the sunlight.

While all rain forests share these common features, the specific plants and animals that live in them differ greatly from one geographical area to another. The largest rain forest, the Amazon basin of South America, holds more plant and animal species than anywhere else on earth—one-fifth to one-third of all flowering plants, up to half the world's birds, and no one knows how many insects, though recent estimates have ranged as high as 30 million species. One Amazonian lake about the size of two tennis courts was found to contain two hundred species of fish, more kinds than in all the rivers of Europe combined.

To learn how you can help preserve and protect the wonderful animals and plants of the rain forest, you might want to visit the Rainforest Action Network at http://www.ran.org/, or write to: Rainforest Action Network, 221 Pine St., Suite 500, San Francisco, CA 94104.

Or you might want to find out about Bosque Eterno de los Niños, a very special rain forest that has been preserved entirely by the efforts of children from around the world. To learn more, visit http://www.google.com and type in: "Children's Eternal Rain Forest." Or write to: Monteverde Conservation League and Children's Eternal Rain Forest, Apartado 10581-1000 San José, Costa Rica, America Central; E-mail: acmmcl@racsa.co.cr.

With love to

Brynn Elizabeth Snowflower Doughty

Hayden Bryanna Sunflower Doughty

Bryson Vincent FallingStar Doughty

—S.K.

The publisher gratefully thanks Dr. Scott Silver, Curator of Animals at
the Queens Zoo, The Wildlife Conservation Society, for his kind assistance.

Pastels were used to create the full-color art.
The text type is Maiandra GD.

Library of Congress Cataloging-in-Publication Data

Katz, Susan.
Looking for jaguar and other rain forest poems / by Susan Katz ;
pictures by Lee Christiansen.
p. cm.
"Greenwillow Books."
ISBN 0-06-029791-3 (trade). ISBN 0-06-029793-X (lib. bdg.)
1. Rain forests—Juvenile poetry. 2. Nature—Juvenile poetry. 3. Children's poetry, American.
I. Title: Looking for jaguar. II. Christiansen, Lee, ill. III. Title.
PS3561.A775L66 2005 811'.54—dc22 2004042407

First Edition 10 9 8 7 6 5 4 3 2 1
 Greenwillow Books